Beyond the Sea

Beyond the Sea

Kristen Da Silva

Beyond the Sea
first published 2024 by Scirocco Drama
An imprint of J. Gordon Shillingford Publishing Inc.
© 2024 Kristen Da Silva

Scirocco Drama Editor: Glenda MacFarlane
Cover design by Doowah Design
Author photo by Patrick Hodgson
Production photos by J.P. Antonacci and Michael Green

Printed and bound in Canada on 100% post-consumer recycled paper.

Performance inquiries to:
Colin Rivers, Managing Literary Agent
Marquis Literary
10 Adelaide Street East, Suite 402
Toronto, Ontario M5C 1J3
416-960-9123 x 223
info@mqlit.ca

Library and Archives Canada Cataloguing in Publication

Title: Beyond the sea / Kristen Da Silva.
Names: Da Silva, Kristen, author.
Identifiers: Canadiana 20240358139 | ISBN 9781990738326 (softcover)
Subjects: LCGFT: Drama.
Classification: LCC PS8607.A18 B49 2024 | DDC C812/.6—dc23

We acknowledge the financial support of the Canada Council for the Arts, the Government of Canada, the Manitoba Arts Council, and the Manitoba Government for our publishing program.

J. Gordon Shillingford Publishing
P.O. Box 86, RPO Corydon Avenue, Winnipeg, MB Canada R3M 3S3

For Nelson

I'll meet you at the sea

Kristen Da Silva

Kristen Da Silva was born in Oakville, Ontario and raised in Nobleton, Ontario, a small farming community in King Township. She graduated from York University and continued her studies at Sheridan College.

Her plays, which include *Where You Are* (Scirocco Drama, 2022), *Hurry Hard*, *The Rules of Playing Risk*, *Sugar Road* and *Beyond the Sea*, are set in Ontario locales from Sudbury to Stayner and have been produced in provinces across Canada, in the United States, Italy and Germany. She is a two-time recipient of the Playwrights Guild New Comedy award.

Kristen works as an actor and writer.

Acknowledgements

Colin Rivers and the team at Marquis Literary.

Lighthouse Festival Theatre, which commissioned and premiered this play, with special thanks to Artistic Director Derek Ritschel; the cast: Jane Spence and Jeffrey Wetsch; and the designers, crew and administrators who brought it to the stage.

Dean Patrick Fleming and Hudson Theatre.

Nelson, Luke, Virginia and Jude.

Foreword

When I think back on the time during which *Beyond the Sea* was being imagined, I am struck by how emotionally raw the world was. Covid was a giant in our lives. Family became so much more precious. Time with friends was careful; yet sometimes recklessly embraced. Each and every second with others was a gift. We listened more deeply. We shared. We laughed and cried … without judgment. We truly embraced one another for who we are.

This is the emotional world in which Gwen and Theo exist. Two souls travelling through the cosmos. Each destination endlessly distant from the other. One is searching. One has embraced the boundary. One grapples with doubt, in themselves and the world. One rests in a cathartic inevitable. The distance between them … immeasurable.

However, *Beyond the Sea* shares with us that no matter how far two souls stand apart, however vast an ocean of darkness stands between them, two people with but a glimpse of compassion and openness can traverse any distance the mind has constructed. There will be struggle, there will be battle, there will be laughter and tears, but there will be someone with you, if you let them.

I have seen this show play in theatres with the full complement of lights, set, and sounds. I have seen it play out in the elements with only a sunset to accentuate time. I have seen it play out under a simple tent and each and every time I experience it, I marvel at how engaged and enthralled the audience is with these two lost souls.

The power of the spoken word is often lost in today's flashy entertainment world, rife with mind-numbing special effects and pageantry. *Beyond the Sea* effortlessly cuts through these trappings. It returns us to the spoken word, our emotions and a human connection that can overcome the vast distances on Gwen and Theo's tiny pier.

Derek Ritschel
Artistic Director, Lighthouse Festival Theatre

Production History

Beyond the Sea was commissioned and produced by Lighthouse Festival Theatre in August 2021, with the following creative team:

Gwen: ....Jane Spence

Theo: ....Jeffrey Wetsch

Directed by: ....Derek Ritschel

Stage Manager:................................. Daniele Guillaume

Set Design: .... Hailey Parker

Costume Design:.. Alice Barnett

Gwen (Jane Spence) looks on as Theo (Jeffrey Wetsch) recounts the story of his marriage. Lighthouse Festival Theatre, 2021. Photo by J.P. Antonacci.

Gwen (Jane Spence) and Theo (Jeffrey Wetsch) look out on the water. Lighthouse Festival Theatre, 2021. Photo by J.P. Antonacci.

Gwen (Julie Tamiko Manning) regales Theo (Quincy Armorer) with an embarrassing story. Hudson Village Theatre, 2023, directed by Dean Patrick Fleming, set and lighting by Peter Vatsis, costumes by Rachel Quintero Faia. Photo by Michael Green.

Gwen (Julie Tamiko Manning) calls out to the boat while Theo (Quincy Armorer) watches. Hudson Village Theatre, 2023, directed by Dean Patrick Fleming, set and lighting by Peter Vatsis, costumes by Rachel Quintero Faia. Photo by Michael Green.

Characters

Gwen: ....In her forties

Theo: ....In his forties

The playwright encourages diverse casting.

Production Note

The playwright intends that this play be performed straight through, without an intermission; however, if necessary, an intermission may be placed as indicated in the script.

Setting

Time: The present. Summer. Almost four o'clock.

Place: A pier. There is a wooden kiosk or stand. A sandwich board reads "The Woman in White" and, underneath that, "Ghost Boat Tour." A bench sits nearby.

At rise, GWEN, dressed in a 19th-century costume, stands by the kiosk. She looks around and then hikes up her skirt to cool her legs. THEO enters. They see one another. She drops the skirt.

GWEN: It's wool. *(Beat.)* How can I help you?

THEO: Uh…Could you tell me what time the boat tour—

GWEN: One o'clock, four o'clock and seven o'clock.

THEO: Oh. So, if someone were to miss the four o'clock the only other one today is at seven?

GWEN: That's right.

THEO: Great.

GWEN: Did you want to buy a ticket?

THEO: Pardon?

GWEN: A ticket. Do you want one? Everyone else has already boarded.

THEO: No. No. I have a ticket.

GWEN: Okay. *(A beat.)* Are you going to board?

THEO: Uh, no.

GWEN: You're not.

THEO: No.

GWEN: Well, just so you know, you don't have a lot
             of time.

THEO: I'm aware.

                     He sits.

GWEN: Okay then.

                     A long beat.

THEO: Wool?

GWEN: One hundred percent.

THEO: Do these ghost boat tours run in the winter?

GWEN: May to September.

THEO: ...and wool?

GWEN: Wool.

THEO: I'm sorry.

GWEN: Thanks.

                     *THEO checks his phone and gestures
                     incredulously upon seeing he has no new
                     messages. GWEN takes out a book. A long
                     beat.*

THEO: Is that any good?

GWEN: What?

THEO: Your book. I just finished mine.

GWEN: I don't know. I'm not really reading it. I just
             hold it to deter men from talking to me.

THEO: Oh, smart. Does it work?

GWEN: Hit and miss.

THEO: Some people have no self-awareness. *(Beat.)* Oh. I see. This is— I'm the man talking to you.

GWEN: Currently, yes.

THEO: Sorry.

GWEN: It's fine.

Beat.

THEO: Just to clarify, I'm not trying to…

GWEN: What?

THEO: I'm not…you know, hitting on you.

GWEN: That's good to know.

THEO: No, really. I'm actually waiting for a date. She's taking the ferry over. Or she will be taking the ferry over. It's apparently broken down.

GWEN: I see.

THEO: I'd wait over there but there's no shade.

GWEN: Right.

A long beat.

THEO: I have a mole my doctor doesn't like.

GWEN: What?

THEO: That's why I need to stay out of the sun. *(Beat.)* It has an irregular shape. That's bad.

GWEN: I've heard that.

THEO: I'm not hitting on you.

GWEN: I hope not, because you're talking about your mole a lot.

THEO: Yeah, I am. Sorry. I'll let you get back to not reading your book.

GWEN: Thanks. I might actually. It was a bestseller.

> *THEO checks his phone. He unbuttons a button on his shirt. A beat. He buttons it back up. Repeat. He stares at his shoes and makes a noise of misery. GWEN hears but ignores it. He holds up his foot and makes another noise.*

Are you injured?

THEO: What?

GWEN: You're groaning like you're injured. Do you need a paramedic?

THEO: No, I'm not injured.

GWEN: Glad to hear it.

> *A beat.*

THEO: Could I ask you a question?

GWEN: One o'clock, four o'clock and seven o'clock.

THEO: No, not that. You must see a lot of people on dates in your line of work, right?

GWEN: This is not my line of work. This is just a job. But, yes, people love bringing dates on morbid boat tours.

THEO: Morbid?

GWEN: Yeah.

THEO: I don't know if I agree it's "morbid."

GWEN: It's a boat tour about a dead woman.

THEO: It's romantic.

GWEN: Is this a first date?

THEO: Yes.

GWEN: Well, no offence, but, in my opinion, it sets a weird tone. Why not take your date for ice cream? Rent a paddleboat? Something less lugubrious.

THEO: Lugubrious! Wow. You just dropped that into a sentence like it's nothing. Great word.

GWEN: It's underused.

THEO: Agree. And, on the matter of paddleboats, I would argue they're a little expected. Trite, even.

GWEN: Trite?

THEO: Yeah. Dull, unimaginative. *(Beat.)* And I just defined a word for a lady who used "lugubrious" without hesitation.

GWEN: Things become trite because they work.

THEO: That's a fair point.

GWEN: Thank you.

THEO: Anyway, it's about my shoes. The guy who sold them to me called them "statement shoes." I thought they'd make me seem interesting, but the more I look at them, they're just weird.

GWEN: What was the question?

THEO: Are they weird?

GWEN: They're not that weird.

THEO: They're not *that* weird or they're not weird?

GWEN: They're…I don't mind them.

THEO: Really? Even this part?

> *She shrugs.*

What about the shirt? Earlier I felt like taking a risk, and now I feel like that was probably a mistake.

GWEN: You took a risk?

THEO: Yeah.

GWEN: What was it?

THEO: The colour.

GWEN: The colour? It's blue.

THEO: It's purple.

GWEN: No. That's not purple.

THEO: It's a shade of purple.

GWEN: It's a shade of blue.

THEO: Well, it leans purple.

GWEN: Okay, well, I think at the very most, *it's* periwinkle.

THEO: Periwinkle! Is she gonna like that? I don't know. It could be polarizing. Is there a shirt store nearby?

GWEN: A shirt store. Yeah, there's a great place where you can get one that makes it look like your head is on a bikini. Just over there. *(Beat.)* You honestly look fine.

THEO: What?

GWEN: You look fine.

THEO:	*Fine?*
GWEN:	Yes. It's a compliment.
THEO:	No, it's not!
GWEN:	You know what? I'm sorry. I meant to say you look nice. It's a fantastic colour.
THEO:	Really?
GWEN:	Yeah, it's— *(She suddenly turns and hollers to the boat.)* BON VOYAGE, MORTALS! BEWAAARE THE SPIRITS! *(To him.)* Sorry, if I don't do that they write me up.
THEO:	No problem. I should stop distracting you.
GWEN:	Yes. This is not a job with a large margin for error. If I screw it up, whole town: doomed.

> *She goes back to her book. He opens his backpack.*

THEO:	Oh shhh—my baguette! *(He pulls out a baguette with a serious bend in it.)* Fuuu— Nice one, Theo, ya big…

> *He breaks off a piece of bread and is about to throw it to the ducks.*

GWEN:	Oh, don't—
THEO:	What?
GWEN:	Don't give that to the ducks.
THEO:	Sorry, did you want some?
GWEN:	No, but it's not good for them. Or the lake.
THEO:	It's just a little piece.

GWEN: Well, that's what everyone thinks, but, see everything you do has an impact. Plus, if ten people throw in "just a little piece" today, that's not just a little piece anymore, it's a loaf, so—

THEO: Okay. *(Beat.)* You're really into ducks, huh?

GWEN: Conservation.

        THEO deals with his bread. A beat.

THEO: I want you to know I recycle.

GWEN: What?

THEO: Every week. Blue bin. Sometimes I recycle things I'm not even entirely sure are recyclable.

GWEN: Who doesn't?

THEO: What's the call on paper towel?

GWEN: Compost.

THEO: Good to know. Listen, I'm not indifferent to the ducks. I didn't know about the bread. I love ducks. All of them. Donald, especially. *(Beat.)* You're big into the environment?

GWEN: Yeah, that's why I dress this way. I only buy handmade clothes from the 1800s.

THEO: You're very committed.

GWEN: Yeah. Kidding aside, though, we should all be "big into the environment." It's one of the things we should be biggest into. I mean, if the earth becomes uninhabitable, what difference do our other problems make?

THEO: Another good point.

He walks and then pauses.

Do you hear that?

GWEN: What?

THEO: It's my shoes. Listen. *(He walks.)* Squeak, squeak, squeak. You don't hear that?

GWEN: No.

THEO: They're squeaking! Listen.

He walks.

GWEN: Nothing.

THEO: Alright. It's probably in my head.

He walks back to the bench.

GWEN: What's that squeaking noise?

THEO: What? I told you!

GWEN: I'm messing with you. Your shoes are fine.

THEO: Oh God!

GWEN: I mean, volume-wise. They're silent. You could be a mime.

THEO: Thank you.

Back to her book. After a moment:

GWEN: Oh, SCREW YOU! *(Beat. To him.)* Oh, no, not you.

THEO: Are you okay?

GWEN: I'm just angry about how much I hate this book.

THEO: Didn't you just start it?

GWEN: Yes, and listen to how he introduces the lead character. "She was gorgeous but didn't know it."

THEO: Hm.

GWEN: First of all, could someone be gorgeous and not know it? Second of all, what point is he trying to make? She has to atone for her appearance? She has to be clueless about her own gorgeousness, because if she admitted she was gorgeous it would be some kind of character flaw?

THEO: It does seem unlikely. Does she not have a mirror?

GWEN: Even if she had no mirror, I'm sure someone would have let her in on it at some point. *(She reads further.)* Oh my God.

THEO: What?

GWEN: "As Spurgeon set eyes on her, he gasped, 'I've never seen a forensic botanist with a body like that!'"

THEO: Ugh.

GWEN: Gag me! Stick your finger right down my throat!

THEO: That's bad. That was a bestseller?

GWEN: Bestseller.

THEO: No accounting for taste.

GWEN: Nope.

THEO: And did you say Spurgeon?

GWEN: Yeah.

THEO:	Is that his name?
GWEN:	Yeah. He's a British spy.
THEO:	Isn't spurgeon a kind of fish?
GWEN:	Sturgeon.
THEO:	What's a spurgeon?
GWEN:	I don't think it's anything.
THEO:	Throw that thing in the trash.
GWEN:	You don't like the name Spurgeon?
THEO:	No, do you?
GWEN:	Well, it's my name, so…
THEO:	Oh God.
GWEN:	I'm joking. My name's Gwen. Which is here, on my name tag.
THEO:	Oh. Heh. That's…thanks, that was a fun couple seconds. Gwen, that's nice. Short for Gwendolyn?
GWEN:	Gwenjamin.
THEO:	Gwenjamin?
GWEN:	Like Benjamin?
THEO:	Right. That's…pretty.
GWEN:	It's short for Gwendolyn.
THEO:	Comedian, huh?
GWEN:	Gotta find some way to entertain myself.
THEO:	I'm not going to fall for it again, Gwenjamin.

GWEN: No?

THEO: I'm on to you.

GWEN: Alright. Well, it's nice to meet you too…

THEO: Theo.

GWEN: No, really.

THEO: It's really Theo.

GWEN: *Theo.* Come on. It was funny when I did it—

THEO: Is there something wrong with Theo?

GWEN: *Theo?* Like with a T?

THEO: Yes, with a T. You've never heard it before?

GWEN: Spell it?

THEO: T-H-E— Oh, you—

GWEN: It's like taking candy from a baby. *(Beat.)* Theo's a nice name. I like it.

THEO: Thank you.

                     He checks his phone and groans.

GWEN: First aid building is attached to the public washrooms.

THEO: I'm sorry, it's just, my date hasn't texted me an update since she told me about the ferry. Do you think she's mad at me?

GWEN: Didn't you say this was your first date?

THEO: Yeah.

GWEN: Then how could she be mad at you?

THEO:	I don't know, I'm just wondering why she hasn't texted me. I sent my reply forty minutes ago. What did I write? *(He reads it.)* "It'll be worth the wait. Hope you're hungry." And I did this emoji of the two high fives.
GWEN:	That's a hug.
THEO:	What?
GWEN:	It's not two high fives. It's a hug.
THEO:	It is?
GWEN:	Yeah.
THEO:	I sent a hug?
GWEN:	Yes.
THEO:	We're strangers!
GWEN:	Well, not after that text.
THEO:	Holy crap. This is bad, right?
GWEN:	Are you being serious right now? What you wrote was fine. She's not mad at you.
THEO:	Yeah, you're probably right.
GWEN:	Are you always this…
THEO:	Neurotic? No. *(Beat.)* Yes. What? Why are you smiling like that?
GWEN:	Nothing.
THEO:	No, what?
GWEN:	It's bloody endearing.
THEO:	It's endearing?

GWEN: Yeah. Because you actually seem to care about meeting this person. And how often do you see that anymore?

THEO: Endearing is a real step up from fine.

GWEN: I think so.

THEO: "What's Theo like?" "He's fine." What's Theo like?" "He's endearing." *(Beat.)* "Weird shoes though."

GWEN: You're thinking way too much about the shoes.

THEO: I know. *(Beat.)* This is gonna sound…out there, but I have this feeling. I've been having it all day. I'm sorry, why am I telling you this? You don't care.

GWEN: What kind of feeling?

THEO: Hard to explain. Kind of a queasy feeling.

GWEN: Well, might I suggest rethinking the boat tour?

THEO: No, like…butterflies, I guess. It's like today I'm on a crash course with something really important. Like it's not just another day in my life. It's a turning point.

GWEN: You woke up feeling all that?

THEO: Yeah. I don't know when I even started believing in that. Maybe I'm eating too much kale.

GWEN: Believing in what?

THEO: Soulmates.

GWEN: Soulmates exist.

THEO: What?

GWEN: Maybe we don't always find them, and maybe they don't always appear as lovers, but they exist. *(She suddenly turns and hollers.)* IF YOU SEE THE WOMAN IN WHITE, TURN AWAY, DON'T LOOK UPON HER FAAACE! *(Turning back.)* I'm so sorry.

THEO: No, that's fine. I'm disturbing you. You must have things to do, right?

GWEN: While it is a very demanding job, all I really have to do right now is count these tickets and balance them against this printout, but since there are only *(She checks.)* eight people onboard, I don't think it's gonna take me long. *(Beat.)* There, I'm done.

THEO: That's all you have to do?

GWEN: I'm also supposed to wave this sign around, but I never do that. *(She shows him a giant arrow with GHOST BOAT TOUR written on it.)*

THEO: Okay, then can I tell you something else? There's this book series, Witness in Time. It's one of my favourite things ever, since I was a kid. My dad always said that, if I ever managed to meet a woman who liked the books, I'd have to marry her. Last night, I found out that the woman I'm meeting today is a huge fan. She's read all nine, even *Return to—*

GWEN: *Tomorrow's Yesterday?* Wow. I could barely finish that one.

THEO: Whaat? You've read the Witness in Time series?

GWEN: Yeah. She likes those books?

THEO:	Loves them.
GWEN:	Well, she has good taste.
THEO:	I can't believe it! *(Beat.)* Wait a minute. You're not…Your name's not actually Erica, is it?
GWEN:	It's Gwen. We just did this.
THEO:	I know, I just thought maybe this has all been an elaborate prank. It feels like something you'd do.
GWEN:	You've known me less than twenty minutes.
THEO:	And I've learned a lot.
GWEN:	So you think, what? That I killed the woman who really does this job so I could steal her costume to impress you with my wit on our first date?
THEO:	Well, when you go that far with it…
GWEN:	I'm not pranking you. I'm not your date. My name is actually Gwen and this is actually my life. *(To someone passing offstage.)* Hey, excuse me, you dropped your coffee cup. Do you want me to throw that out for you? You seem like you're in a hurry. Garbage is over there. *(To THEO.)* Sorry, what were we talking about?
THEO:	Just how funny it would be if you were actually my date.
GWEN:	Yeah, imagine you were worried about your shirt and then I showed up in this, looking like I'm about to accuse you of witchcraft.
THEO:	It's not bad.
GWEN:	Stop it.

THEO:	No, I mean it, you look good. You look like you'd make delicious butter.

She mimes churning butter and he notices the ring on her finger.

Ah, you're married. Right. One more reason you couldn't be my date. Cool to find out you're a fan of Witness in Time, though. *(A beat.)* Huh.

GWEN:	What?
THEO:	I was reading a lot of significance into her liking those books. And then you also like them. That guy over there with the Frisbee could be the world's biggest fan, for all I know, and he's not my soulmate. I hate Frisbee.
GWEN:	Maybe she's your soulmate, maybe she's not. I would suggest shaking her hand and going from there.
THEO:	Are you and your husband soulmates?
GWEN:	Oh, uh…
THEO:	Whoa, sorry, that's super intense. "Hey, nice to meet ya, is your husband your soulmate?" I mean, what if he's not? Awkward for you. Not that I would tell him you said that, if I ever met him. Why would I meet him?
GWEN:	You couldn't.
THEO:	Oh, is…
GWEN:	He died.
THEO:	I'm so sorry. What an asshole! *(Beat.)* Me! Not him! I'm…God rest his soul.

GWEN: Thank you.

THEO: I'm really sorry.

GWEN: It's really okay. *(Beat.)* And yes. The answer is yes.

THEO: Sorry, the answer to?

GWEN: You asked if we were soulmates. I think we were.

THEO: Really? That's beautiful. If you don't mind me asking, how long has he been…?

GWEN: What?

THEO: You know…

GWEN: Dead? Are you afraid to say dead?

THEO: Yeah. Is there a nicer term? Do you prefer passed away?

GWEN: No, not particularly.

THEO: "Dead" just seems very blunt. What about "in a better place"?

GWEN: Well, that sort of supposes I agree, and I don't. You can call it whatever you want, but don't do it on my account. It doesn't change the fact that he's not here anymore

THEO: No, it doesn't. I'm sorry.

GWEN: Thank you. And it'll be two years tomorrow.

             Beat. A sound from his phone.

             Oh, your phone.

THEO: It's Erica!

             He checks.

GWEN:	Not her?
THEO:	No, but I can get a family roaming plan for just eighty-five dollars a month.

A long beat.

Maybe she's not coming.

GWEN:	Or maybe they haven't fixed the ferry yet.
THEO:	Maybe. *(Beat.)* This is my first date in eleven years.
GWEN:	Eleven years!
THEO:	I was married for most of those.
GWEN:	Oh. Are you...
THEO:	Divorced? Are you afraid to say divorced?
GWEN:	Touché. Is there a nicer term?
THEO:	No.
GWEN:	Sorry to hear.
THEO:	Thanks. I might've had it coming.
GWEN:	What?
THEO:	The divorce.
GWEN:	And why's that?
THEO:	Long story. But the short version is I was a jerk.
GWEN:	You seem like an alright guy to me.
THEO:	Thanks, I appreciate that, because I've spent the last year and a half trying to become one. But, when I was with Naomi, I doubt anyone would've described me that way.

GWEN:	You don't know that.
THEO:	I have a pretty good idea. In fact, the same day she left I got fired from my job. Ten years as the top salesperson in the company. Imagine my surprise. Did they not like money? Were shareholders complaining they were getting too rich? But it turned out it had nothing to do with my numbers. Because, as my boss, who was also the best man at our wedding, had to break it to me, nobody there could stand me. Including him.
GWEN:	Jeez.
THEO:	Turns out ruthlessness is an unlikable quality. So, there I was packing up my desk as Naomi was packing up her things at home. Still hate the smell of cardboard.
GWEN:	I guess we all have our rock bottom.
THEO:	Oh, that wasn't my rock bottom.
GWEN:	No?
THEO:	No. My rock bottom was a month later at my nephew's pool party.
GWEN:	What happened?
THEO:	Nah. I don't want to—
GWEN:	Come on. You can't just dangle something like that. Do you have any idea how boring this job is? Anyway, what difference does it make? You're never going to see me again. And unless hearing this story puts me in a moral obligation to report you to the police…
THEO:	What?

GWEN:
: I don't know. Maybe it's a story about you teaching swimsuit-clad children to launder money.

THEO:
: It's not.

GWEN:
: Are you sure?

Beat.

THEO:
: I was in the running for a new job. A great job, at a competing company. I wanted it bad. Mostly to prove to John-Paul—

GWEN:
: Wait. Who's John-Paul?

THEO:
: My former boss.

GWEN:
: Well, I don't know that. You can't just throw a name at me. You have to introduce new characters with proper exposition. John-Paul could be your ear-nose-and-throat doctor for all I know.

THEO:
: You think I wanted to prove something to my ear-nose-and-throat doctor?

GWEN:
: It's possible. I barely know you.

THEO:
: John-Paul was my boss.

GWEN:
: The one who was the best man at your wedding.

THEO:
: Correct.

GWEN:
: Where were we?

THEO:
: Pool party. New job.

GWEN:
: Right. What happened?

THEO:	A call came in from the recruiter, mid-party. I was trying to take it but, I don't know if you've ever been to a kids' pool party—
GWEN:	I have not.
THEO:	It is literally the loudest place on earth. There was so much screaming I could barely hear this woman, never mind tell her I was perfect for the job. Long story short, I lost my temper. I screamed. And then I chucked my phone into the pool and I stabbed a narwhal in the face.
GWEN:	They got your nephew a narwhal?!
THEO:	It was a vinyl narwhal, a pool toy. You think I'd stab a living narwhal?
GWEN:	You said rock bottom.
THEO:	God.
GWEN:	So, it was a plastic narwhal.
THEO:	Yes, and it was very cute...until I harpooned it in the eye with a barbeque fork. At which point, the five-year-olds came undone.

She starts to laugh. He starts to laugh.

	That was that party over, and they hadn't even delivered the pizza yet. My sister asked me to leave, and she used some very harsh expletives.
GWEN:	I'm sorry.
THEO:	It's funny now, but at the time...I felt more ashamed than I'd ever felt my entire life. The next morning, I cashed my severance cheque

and decided to take a year off. Figure out what the hell had happened to me. Maybe if I'd done that earlier I'd still have my life.

GWEN: Maybe.

                A beat.

THEO: That's funny.

GWEN: What?

THEO: Whenever I say something like that to my friends or family they always come back with something like "It was all for the best" or "Things happen for a reason."

GWEN: I hate when people say that.

THEO: Me too.

GWEN: Did your year off help?

THEO: Watched a lot of Netflix.

GWEN: Yeah.

THEO: And thought. Did a lot of thinking. I don't know. I think I'm a better person now. I hope I am.

GWEN: Next-gen Theo?

THEO: Yep. And he wears periwinkle. And gets stood up.

GWEN: You aren't being stood up. The ferry's delayed.

THEO: Is it, though?

GWEN: Yes!

THEO:	You know what, just to be sure, I'm going to send her another text.
GWEN:	Why don't you just call her?
THEO:	Call her? What, like with my voice?
GWEN:	Yeah.
THEO:	No. I can't do that.
GWEN:	Why?
THEO:	Because no one calls anyone anymore, except grandmas and dentist offices. It would be weird. *(He gets ready to compose a text.)* Okay...What do I say? "Hey Erica... I guess the ferry is still delayed. I'm awaiting your arrival and hope I will soon be...in your beautiful presence." *(Beat.)* Is that too much?
GWEN:	It depends. Which century will she be receiving it in?
THEO:	Yeah, it's too flowery. Uh. "I await the tardy ferry with bated breath."
GWEN:	Still. Do you talk like that in real life?
THEO:	"Hey Erica. Still looking forward to our date. Let me know how things are going with the ferry."
GWEN:	Perfect.
THEO:	Good.
	He hits send. A beat. His phone dings.
	Oh, she responded. *(He reads.)* "K."
GWEN:	K?
THEO:	The letter "k."

GWEN: That's it?

THEO: That's it.

GWEN: That can't be it.

THEO: It is it.

GWEN: Just "k"?

THEO: "K."

GWEN: Does she mean "OK"?

THEO: I assume she's means "OK."

GWEN: Huh.

THEO: She didn't type "OK," though. I wrote three drafts of my text to her.

GWEN: Yeah.

THEO: And she can't even type out the whole word? It's two letters. And they're right by each other!

GWEN: At least she spelled it right.

THEO: Oh no, I don't like this.

GWEN: No. Or as she would say, "o." Let's give her the benefit of the doubt. Maybe her hands aren't free.

THEO: Yeah, maybe she's swimming over. And she didn't give me an update on the ferry. Are they fixing it? Is it on its way? It's anyone's guess.

GWEN: So she's not good with text. You know, maybe that's alright. People rely on it too much anyway.

THEO: Yeah.

                    A long beat.

               You okay?

GWEN: Yeah, I was just thinking about the last text I
               sent Nate, my husband.

THEO: What was it?

GWEN: It was about the Tupperware lids.

THEO: Couldn't find a match?

GWEN: No. And that was the last thing I said to him
               on this earth. And he was so romantic too.
               Our whole marriage. I think about that stupid
               text a lot. What an insignificant thing to say.
               (Beat. To someone offstage.) Hey, I think you
               missed the garbage can! It's on the other side
               of you. Easy mistake. *(To THEO.)* Sorry.

THEO: Slobs.

GWEN: Makes me angry.

THEO: Does it bother you to talk about?

GWEN: Littering?

THEO: Your husband. Nate. Does it bring back sad
               feelings?

GWEN: They don't leave. They never leave. *(Beat.)* So,
               what's Erica like? Tell me about her.

THEO: Uh, well, I don't know that much. We've only
               had a couple of quick conversations through
               the app.

GWEN: What does she do?

THEO: She's a researcher. She's working on quantum
               lasers.

GWEN: Wow. Quantum lasers. Not even just regular lasers.

THEO: Anyway, I thought the ghost boat tour would be up her alley.

GWEN: Well, there's no lasers, I can tell you right now.

He looks at the brochure.

THEO: "The Woman in White, a haunting tale. Fully licensed bar." I guess you must know all about the legend.

GWEN: A beautiful woman threw herself into the sea and now she haunts the waterfront in her nightgown.

THEO: The river. She threw herself into the river. See? "As the river flows to the lake and the lake flows to the sea..." You should go sometime.

GWEN: I think I'll pass.

THEO: Oh God. Of course you don't want to go. I'm so sorry, Gwen.

GWEN: What are you talking about?

THEO: The whole thing is about death.

GWEN: It's okay, Theo. I work here.

THEO: Right.

GWEN: You need to relax. *(She turns and hollers.)* STARE STRAIGHT AHEAD, NEVER STRAY! THE GHOUL WAITS FOR THOSE WHO CAN'T RESIIIST! *(To him.)* Do they not realize they're just going in circles?

THEO:	Suspension of disbelief.
GWEN:	What?
THEO:	Our willingness to forgo logic to have an experience.
GWEN:	I've never heard that.
THEO:	You haven't?
GWEN:	Why is that so surprising? You use "lugubrious" one time—
THEO:	Suspension of disbelief is how we can we sit in a theatre and pretend we're really in Verona and the actors on the stage are really living and dying right in front of us.
GWEN:	Maybe that accounts for why we're so tempted by the promise of love.
THEO:	How so?
GWEN:	Well, it always ends, doesn't it? And yet most of us rush in time and time again, pretending this time there won't be a goodbye. But there's always a goodbye. I mean, you're meeting Erica today. Maybe you two will fall in love and somehow make it through all the hurdles, have years together, if you're lucky. But there's going to come a day when one of you will get a phone call. Maybe you'll have time to rush to a bedside where you can hold a frail hand or maybe you won't. Maybe you'll never even get to say the word.

A beat.

THEO:	You know you're really making me second-guess getting back out there.
GWEN:	I'm sorry.

A beat.

THEO: Are you hungry? I have brie. It was supposed to be for the date, but it's going to spoil in this heat.

GWEN: You've had brie this whole time?!

THEO: Yeah.

GWEN: Why am I not already eating it?

He takes a number of food items and picnic accoutrements from his backpack.

What's this?

THEO: Chutney.

GWEN: Chutney. Mango?

THEO: Peach, but it's not my best batch. Try the breadsticks.

GWEN: Mm.

He takes out a bottle of wine.

THEO: I've been saving this. It costs two hundred bucks a bottle.

GWEN: Are you a wine collector?

THEO: No, I won it at a golf tournament. But I've heard it's really good. It should be at that price. *(He feels the glass.)* Does that feel like twelve degrees to you?

She feels the glass.

GWEN: That's really hard to say. My hand thermometer is broken.

THEO: I'm supposed to store it at twelve degrees.

GWEN: *(She checks her phone.)* It's twenty-eight degrees out, but it feels like thirty-four with the humidity. How do they measure that? Is that just the weather guy going outside and saying "Man, it feels hotter than twenty-eight"?

THEO: I think so.

GWEN: If you're worried it's going go bad, open it. You should get to enjoy it.

THEO: I can't drink it alone. I guess you wouldn't be able to join me?

GWEN: Are you kidding? Do this job impaired? Do you know how many lives are at stake?

                    Beat. She gestures for wine. He digs in the backpack for a corkscrew. In the process, he takes out a bundle of notecards with an elastic around them. He opens the wine. She picks up the cards.

               What's this?

THEO: Oh. Let me put those back.

GWEN: Are these crib notes? Did you make crib notes for your date? *(She reads the top one.)* "Don't tell narwhal story." Well, good thing you got that out of your system.

THEO: Come on, don't read those.

GWEN: Please? I really want to.

THEO: They're stupid.

GWEN: I'll tell you something embarrassing about me.

THEO: Like what?

GWEN:	I once went shoe shopping and saw a really cute pair of boots in my size so I put them on and started walking around in them. I was just about to buy them when their owner informed me she had just taken them off to try on some sneakers.
THEO:	You tried on someone else's shoes?
GWEN:	Yeah.
THEO:	That's funny, but not that embarrassing. That could happen to anyone.
GWEN:	Well, I got athlete's foot a week later.
THEO:	Still. Not worthy, sorry.
GWEN:	What would be worthy?
THEO:	I'll know it to hear it.
GWEN:	So, you're going to make me stand here and pitch all my most embarrassing moments to you?
THEO:	If you want to read the cards.
GWEN:	You know, you're right, you are a jerk sometimes. *(Beat.)* Okay. I once ended a phone call with "I love you, drive safe," forgetting that I was talking to someone at the hydro company.
THEO:	Did the exact same thing with my mechanic.
GWEN:	Damn you.
THEO:	Come on, Gwen. That's weak.

She thinks.

GWEN:	I broke my tooth in the middle of a date.

THEO:	Which tooth?
GWEN:	Does it matter?
THEO:	A visible tooth?
GWEN:	A molar. But a piece fell out and I caught it in my hand.
THEO:	Who was the date with?
GWEN:	A person.
THEO:	Which person?

Beat.

GWEN:	My boss.
THEO:	You dated your boss?
GWEN:	No! It was a lunch meeting.
THEO:	Nice try. I want a real story. I want the most tragically embarrassing story of your life.

A long beat.

GWEN:	Alright, I've got one, but it's still a little sensitive, even though I was twelve when it happened, so please don't laugh.
THEO:	Twelve! And you still remember it?
GWEN:	Every day.
THEO:	How bad could it be at twelve?
GWEN:	I begged my mother to let me change schools after it happened. And she seriously considered.
THEO:	No way.

GWEN:	You haven't heard the story.
THEO:	Alright. Let's hear it.
GWEN:	I tell you this, I get to read those cards.
THEO:	Why don't you let me be the judge of that?
GWEN:	Listen. Regardless of your reaction, this story is going to cost me something to tell. Once I've told it I am reading those cards or there's no deal.

Beat.

THEO:	Fine.
GWEN:	I'm gonna need wine.

He pours and hands her a glass.

NOTE: If the play is being staged with an intermission, the playwright suggests it be placed here.

GWEN:	It was my father's birthday party.
THEO:	Where?
GWEN:	A banquet hall. My mother hired a decorator, a band, whole nine yards. It was his fiftieth so it was a big one. At the time, I was enrolled in dance lessons, which I hated.
THEO:	Okay?
GWEN:	Well, a few weeks before the party, my mother decided that, after three months of strip-mall jazz lessons, I was totally ready to perform in public. As a gift to my father on his birthday. In front of all of his guests.
THEO:	Oh dear. How many guests?

GWEN: Irrelevant. *(Beat.)* I wouldn't have done it. I didn't want to do it. But she bribed me with the one thing I wanted most in the world. Horseback riding lessons.

THEO: Go on.

GWEN: So, my dance teacher came up with a routine set to "Let's Hear it for the Boy."

THEO: Great song.

GWEN: My mother had a custom leotard made for the occasion. Covered in sequins with feathers on the bottom.

THEO: The bottom of the leotard?

GWEN: On my bottom. I had feathers protruding from my bottom. I looked like a peacock, if a peacock could be leopard print.

THEO: This is terrible.

GWEN: I haven't even gotten there yet, Theo.

THEO: The leotard isn't the embarrassing part?

GWEN: No!

THEO: Good God. What happened?

GWEN: What happened was, the day of the party arrived, and I wanted to back out. But my mother, God rest her soul, was a woman with single-minded focus when she wanted something. So, she slipped me one of her "nerve" pills.

THEO: What?

GWEN: It was the eighties. Parents weren't held to nearly the same standard.

THEO: No.

GWEN: She sent me to the lobby and told me to wait for it to kick in. She said when I came back, I shouldn't even look at all the people in the crowd. Just ignore them, you know, and dance like no one was watching. Twenty minutes later, I was feeling pretty great. So, I picked up my little boom box and I scissor stepped right into that banquet hall, then I jetéd and I flick-kicked from wall to wall, until sweat was pouring down my face. I knew I was really killing it because, other than my music, you could have heard a pin drop in there. As the song faded out, I took several triumphant bows and then I looked for my mother in the crowd. *(Beat.)* That's when I realized I was in the wrong hall.

THEO: NO!

GWEN: Yes. And the hall I was in was hosting a bar mitzvah. For my classmate.

THEO: Oh, Gwen.

GWEN: He was very flattered.

THEO: I bet. Was anyone else you knew there?

GWEN: Pretty much everyone I knew was there.

THEO: That is—

GWEN: I told you.

THEO: Alright. That was a worthy story.

GWEN: Yeah?

THEO: Yeah. Read at will.

GWEN takes a card out of the bundle.

GWEN: *Who do you most admire?*

THEO: I used to forget to ask people questions about themselves. Bad habit.

GWEN: *(Flipping through.) Where did you go to school? Who was your first crush?* Aw.

THEO: Mine was Cheetara from the Thunder Cats.

GWEN: She was a cartoon.

THEO: I know, but she was cute.

GWEN: Wasn't she a cheetah?

THEO: Yeah.

GWEN: So, your first crush wasn't even human?

THEO: Well, she was kind of human. She had cleavage.

                    They both think about this.

               Why did she have cleavage? *(Beat.)* Who was yours?

GWEN: My first crush?

THEO: Yeah.

GWEN: Gilbert Blythe. Obviously.

THEO: Right.

GWEN: *What are you most afraid of?* That's a heavy question for a first date.

THEO: That's a second date question. See, they're colour-coded. I thought maybe if the first date went well, she'd want to see me again tomorrow and I wouldn't have time to write up new questions.

GWEN: What are the pink questions?

THEO: Third date.

GWEN: Oh, third date! Those are the ones I want to read. *Where was your first kiss? (Beat.)* Wasaga Beach.

THEO: Oh yeah?

GWEN: Summer I turned fifteen. You?

THEO: Canada's Wonderland.

GWEN: Classic.

THEO: Back when they had the Zumba Flume.

GWEN: *(She reads the next card.) What was your best kiss?*

THEO: I'm going to save that for after I kiss her.

GWEN: Smooth.

                    A long beat.

THEO: Where'd you just go?

GWEN: I was just thinking of my best kiss. *(Beat.)* Well, Theo, you've planned for everything.

THEO: Yeah, except what to do when your date doesn't show up.

GWEN: She's going to show up. And when she does, she's gonna have a great time, because you've prepared a really nice date. Of course, she won't get any food. Or wine. But you've still got the boat.

THEO: Yeah, and I'm really looking forward to that.

GWEN: God, it's hot. You have any ice in that bag? I'd like to pour some into my bra.

THEO:	You must be roasting in that.
GWEN:	Under this skirt I'm just a puddle.
THEO:	Are you wearing shorts or something?
GWEN:	No, a petticoat.
THEO:	Is that made of wool?
GWEN:	Cotton.
THEO:	Well, strip down to that. You'd still probably be wearing more clothes than everyone else here.
GWEN:	I can't.
THEO:	Why not?
GWEN:	Because it would spoil the illusion. *(She shows him the petticoat.)* This is the nineteenth-century equivalent of a thong. You'd have marry me if you saw me in this.
THEO:	I saw your bare legs when I walked up. I think, legally, we're already married. Come on, you're going to get heat stroke.
GWEN:	I can't.
THEO:	Why not? What do they pay you, minimum wage?
GWEN:	It doesn't matter. It's still a job that I made a commitment to. In fact, fitting into this costume was pretty much the only qualification. When people pay for a ticket to something like this, they want to see someone dressed in old-timey clothes. It's part of the experience. They don't care that I'm hot or that it's my last day and I can't wait to get out of here.

THEO: It's your last day?

GWEN: Yeah. But it doesn't end until eight.

THEO: That's it? You're done?

GWEN: Yeah, well, after I draft the press release, obviously.

THEO: So, if I come here tomorrow, you won't be here?

GWEN: No, I won't.

THEO: Oh. Well, where are you going next?

GWEN: What?

THEO: After this. You said before this isn't your line of work. Are you going back to your line of work? What is your line of work?

GWEN: Photography. And, no. I'm not. I'm going to travel.

THEO: Oh, that's great. Good for you. Photography?

GWEN: Yeah.

THEO: Can I see some of your photos?

GWEN: I don't have any on me.

THEO: Sure you do.

GWEN: You think I carry my portfolio around?

THEO: You don't have any on your phone?

GWEN: I don't know. Maybe one or two.

THEO: Okay, then show me one or two.

She gives him her phone.

GWEN: It's just this one album. It's only like three hundred shots.

THEO: Wow, Gwen! These are amazing!

GWEN: Thanks. Most of them are pretty old now.

He pauses on one.

THEO: Whoa.

GWEN: That's the Trevi Fountain during a rainstorm. And that's Nate. I saw him sitting there and I watched him awhile, trying to figure out how he could be totally oblivious to the rain streaming down his face.

THEO: He looks like someone grappling with big thoughts.

GWEN: That was Nate. Sadly, me taking his photo seemed to disturb the moment. I thought he might yell at me, but instead he asked if he could see it. Turned out he was a writer there working on an editorial, and the photographer assigned to the job never showed. He looked at the shot and hired me right there.

THEO: I can see why.

GWEN: He also asked me if I'd have dinner with him the next night in Ostia.

THEO: Smooth.

GWEN: He wasn't smooth. He was nervous. When I asked where I should meet him he said, "How about the sea?" as if there aren't miles and miles of seashore. He turned all red. I loved it. From then on, whenever we parted, we didn't say goodbye, we said, "I'll meet you at the sea." *(Beat.)* Oh, I'm sorry.

THEO:	No. Don't be.
GWEN:	Sometimes it just…grabs me by the throat.
THEO:	Yeah.
GWEN:	Are *you* okay?
THEO:	Yeah. I'm fine. Sand.
GWEN:	You got sand in your eye?
THEO:	No. *(Beat.)* That's beautiful, Gwen. "I'll meet you at the sea"? That's beautiful. *(Beat.)* How did he die?
GWEN:	Oh.
THEO:	I'm sorry.
GWEN:	No, it's…He was on an assignment. He had to take a helicopter up into the hills in Virginia. They don't know what happened but the helicopter went down. I knew something was wrong when he didn't text me back about the Tupperware. You know, because even if he was busy, he'd always text something back to make me laugh. I was waiting for that. But instead, I got a call from his editor. No survivors.

They sit there a moment.

THEO:	Would you change it?
GWEN:	What?
THEO:	If you could go back. Would you not meet him at the fountain that day?
GWEN:	What a question.
THEO:	I'm sorry. Is that…It's just, sometimes I wonder if I'd change it.

GWEN: Not go down to the piazza that day and see him there? Not impulsively take his photo in the rain? Say no when he asked me to meet him for dinner? Would I change it? Would I call last minute and say I was sick? Would I turn my head when he leaned to kiss me good night, not catch the scent of his aftershave and feel my knees buckle just a little? Not look him up when I got back to Canada? Never meet his friends, his parents, his dog, find out that he slept nude but with socks and was very particular about how he cut his sandwiches? Say no when he dropped to one knee in Times Square? Look into his eyes as he held my hands in his and not say "I do"?

Lose all those years of laughing, fighting and making up? Of Saturday mornings on our patio? Of Saturday nights in our bed? But also never have to sit in the office of a funeral home, choking on the smell of lilies, while I point to a casket in a catalogue as if I had any idea what the right kind of box was in which to bury the love of my life. Would I change that? I'm going to have to think about that, Theo.

THEO: I'm sorry if I—

GWEN: Would you change it? Would you unmeet Naomi?

THEO: She used to do this voice sometimes. She'd curl up her fingers like this and go, "You're so juicy. I'm gonna eat ya." She'd chase me around the house until I let her catch me and then she'd jump on me, and we'd fall down together, laughing till we cried. No, I don't think I'd change it, even if that's all I ever got, and it isn't. But I do wish she wasn't now married to a craft brewer. *(Beat.)* Listen, I hope I didn't offend you. Sometimes I don't think about things before I—

GWEN: Does he have a beard?

THEO: Who?

GWEN: The craft brewer your ex-wife married.

THEO: Oh. Yeah, of course he has a beard.

GWEN: Shh, shh, shh.

THEO: What?

GWEN: A fox.

THEO: Crap, where?

GWEN: Over there.

THEO: What's he doing out in broad daylight?

GWEN: She, probably, is looking for a meal for her babies. Look at her. Isn't she gorgeous?

THEO: Should I put away the food?

GWEN: No, you're fine.

THEO: Well, what if she comes over here?

GWEN: You think she might march over and demand some chutney?

THEO: I don't know. It's a wild animal.

GWEN: She's more afraid of you than you are of her.

THEO: Doubt that.

GWEN: Oh, look at this guy coming. And there she goes. *(Calling out to someone offstage.)* Hey, you with the phone! You scared her away! What, are you shooting for *National Geographic*? I'm sure that photo you just took on your, what is that, an iPhone 5, is going to be a real winner. *(To THEO.)* Can you believe this guy? He trampled all the flowers. What?

THEO: I've never met anyone like you.

                    Beat.

GWEN: Well, you can relax now. The terrifying omnivore has been chased away.

THEO: Have you seen their teeth? They're very pointy.

GWEN: You grew up in the city.

THEO: Why, because I don't know about foxes?

GWEN: Because you looked like you might scream.

THEO: I wasn't going to scream. But I was poised to protect you if it came to that.

GWEN: Oh, well, thank you. Toronto?

THEO: Yeah. Born and raised. You?

GWEN: Grew up in Caledon. Lived all over with Nate. Landed here after he died.

THEO: Why here?

                    She gestures to the lake, the sky, the view.

             It is beautiful.

GWEN: And quiet. No one knows me here.

THEO: You haven't met anyone?

GWEN: Sure, in passing, but nothing deep enough that I have people I need to notify if I'm going out of town. I don't think anyone here even knows my last name. I make small talk with the bag boys, I wave at the crossing guards, but I don't meet up for lunch. I don't belong to clubs. I don't bring a dish to the church potluck. How about you? How'd you end up so far from the city?

THEO: Naomi's family is all here. And now I'm here, without her. To be honest, I've been on the fence about staying. I keep thinking I should look for a job back in the city. The thing is, I like where I work now. I even have a couple friends there.

GWEN: How long since the divorce?

THEO: Sixteen months.

GWEN: Give it two years. That was our rule. We moved around a lot and liked some places more than others, but we agreed we'd give everything new a fair shot. You need two years after a big change. The first year's a write-off. The second year is when you start to come around, if you're going to.

THEO: Two years?

GWEN: Two years.

THEO: That's a good rule.

GWEN: Yeah.

                        Beat.

THEO: I've run into her at the grocery store a few times.

GWEN: Yikes.

THEO:	Once she was buying the ingredients for a cake she used to make for me. She even called it Theo's Cake. I guess it's Matt's Cake now.
GWEN:	Was he with her?
THEO:	No. Thank God. He has such nice hair.
GWEN:	What?
THEO:	It's lustrous. I used to have good hair.
GWEN:	You still have good hair.
THEO:	No, no. I thought I had okay hair, until I saw Matt's hair. It's like a lion's mane. It has its own Instagram account. And it smells good. You can smell him from across the room.
GWEN:	You follow him on Instagram?
THEO:	I don't follow him. I just go to his page sometimes when I can't sleep.
GWEN:	Does it help?
THEO:	No! It's torture. He gave her a puppy for Christmas. Put it in a giant stocking. There's a video. It's really cute. You know what I gave her the last Christmas we were together? A gift basket I'd bought for my admin assistant. She cried.
GWEN:	The admin assistant?
THEO:	No, Naomi.
GWEN:	What was in the basket?
THEO:	Soap and body lotion.
GWEN:	Oh, Theo.

THEO:	Well, I really didn't know my admin assistant. But I figured she had a body, so she could probably use some lotion for it.
GWEN:	If you ever find yourself handing the woman you love a gift basket of anything, you have taken a wrong turn somewhere.
THEO:	I will keep that in mind for future.
GWEN:	What did the admin assistant get?
THEO:	What?
GWEN:	Well, you gave her gift away.
THEO:	Oh. She got the gift I bought for my accountant.
GWEN:	You bought your accountant a gift but you didn't buy your wife a gift?
THEO:	He's a good accountant.
GWEN:	He must be. So, the admin assistant got…
THEO:	A subscription to *Dividends* magazine.
GWEN:	Festive.
THEO:	I'm an asshole.
GWEN:	You're not an asshole.
THEO:	I ruined Christmas for three people.
GWEN:	I really doubt not getting a gift from you ruined your accountant's Christmas.
THEO:	Well, I ruined Naomi's. The look on her face when she saw that basket… It killed me.
GWEN:	Wow, Theo.

THEO: What?

GWEN: You just shrunk two inches talking about that. How often do you do that?

THEO: What?

GWEN: Ruminate on your mistakes.

THEO: "Ruminate." I don't know. A lot.

GWEN: Well, stop it.

THEO: You can't just stop thinking about your mistakes. If you do that you might forget them.

GWEN: God forbid.

THEO: You think it's that easy? Just forget about everything? I can't. I lost my whole life and it was my fault. It was...me.

GWEN: What exactly happened?

THEO: It's a long story.

GWEN: I'm in the middle of a long shift. Did you abuse her in some way?

THEO: No! Of course not.

GWEN: Then what?

                A long beat.

THEO: I neglected her. I sold her a false bill of goods. Because, before we got married, we used to be great together. We used to laugh all the time. Everywhere. Everywhere we went, no matter what we were doing, it was fun. I was her hero and she was my angel. But something changed when we got married.

People are so good at complicating things. Like housework. What's to fight about? It needs to get done. Nobody wants to live in a dump. But you buy a kitchen together and, suddenly, you're enemies. You can't laugh anymore because you just had your weekly screaming match about wiping down the counter. You've taken sides. You're on the side of "It's just a few crumbs" and she's on the side of "I can't live like this anymore." And later, when she cracks a joke to try to lighten the mood, you want to smile but you begrudge her that because you're still angry. And she notices you don't smile and it makes her not crack the joke next time. It doesn't take long before you're living in a house where no one laughs. So, what do you do then? What you should do is get over yourself and say sorry. Sorry for being petty and childish. But what you do is you double down. You shake the toast a little as you're putting it on your plate so a few more crumbs fall on the counter. After all, she brought your car back on empty the day before which is surely an act of aggression. Now you're not the source of one another's happiness anymore, so you've got to find other things. Buy other things. You buy things. You plant a five-hundred-dollar ornamental tree in your front yard. Why? I don't know. Those trees are a terrible investment. It's like buying a sofa that might not make it through the winter. But you pay for it and it makes you happy for ten minutes. Then you've got to buy something else. A camper, so you can not talk to each other in different locations. And, of course, buying all of these things, having this endless list of wants, helps justify working all the time. It justifies the late nights, the customer dinners that replace dinners together. That's how it went. I worked more and more, never turned down an opportunity to put money in the bank. Sure, I sold more lubricants than—

GWEN: I'm sorry, what?

THEO: I was a salesperson.

GWEN: Yes. For what?

THEO: Lubricants.

GWEN: Lubricants?

THEO: Industrial lubricants. For machines. You know, I was in the middle of kind of a thing there.

GWEN: I know. I'm very sorry. But you can't just say "lubricants" without explanation.

THEO: I worked for a lubricant company. The point I was trying to make was, we lost touch with each other. I became a workaholic. She was lonely. And heartbroken. Because we'd once had such a beautiful thing.

GWEN: That's really sad.

THEO: Yeah.

GWEN: Your parents have a good marriage?

THEO: They had a quiet marriage. An inscrutable marriage.

GWEN: My parents fought.

THEO: I never heard mine fight, but one night I came downstairs and my mom was standing in front of the china cabinet dropping her teacups on the tile floor one by one.

GWEN: Really?

THEO: Yeah. When I walked in, she just looked at me, said nothing and went to bed.

GWEN: You think she was unhappy?

THEO: I don't think she was redecorating.

GWEN: Mine used to play music when they fought. They thought it drowned them out. Didn't. I swore if I got married, we weren't going to fight. And I'm proud to say we never did. Not once.

THEO: Really?

GWEN: No, Theo. We fought all the time. That's normal. Marriage is incredibly hard. That's why so many don't make it. They're not worse people. It's not a moral failing.

THEO: What did you fight about?

GWEN: You name it. Counters, bathrooms, banana stickers, kids.

THEO: What?

GWEN: He'd stick the sticker that comes on the banana to whatever was nearby when he was eating it. What kind of person does that?

THEO: No, you said *"kids."*

GWEN: We fought about kids. And that is a tough issue to find a compromise on. You can't have half a kid. Or have kids occasionally. Kids are an all-in situation.

THEO: You didn't discuss kids before getting married?

GWEN: No. We didn't, because we were in love and we thought that conquered all. I assumed we were on the same page because our lifestyle wasn't conducive to having a family. We moved a lot. Nate travelled. I would have been on my own most of the time. Tied down. I couldn't have pursued my own career.

THEO: Photography.

GWEN: Right. Which was mostly weddings. No one wants kids at a wedding. They have no volume button and most of them don't like shrimp. I'm sure it's all great, don't get me wrong. When you have help. When you have support. When it doesn't mean giving up everything it means to be you, like you're just some pod that only exists to spawn new humans.

THEO: You're still a little mad about this.

GWEN: I wanted to make him happy. And I actually like kids. I just didn't want them in those circumstances. It looks hard enough as it is. And thank God we didn't have any. They'd be orphans now.

THEO: No, they wouldn't. They'd have their mother.

GWEN: They'd wish they were orphans.

THEO: That's crap, Gwen.

GWEN: What?

THEO: It's fine that you don't want to be a mother, but don't disparage yourself. If you had wanted kids, you'd be a great mother. You're wise. You're caring. And you're a hell of a lot of fun. A kid'd be lucky to have you.

GWEN: Thank you.

THEO: You're welcome. I mean it. *(Beat.)* You think there are people out there who have no regrets?

GWEN: If there are, I don't want to know them. Everyone decent has regrets. But you can't do anything about the past. Life moves in one direction.

THEO: I know.

> *A beat. She picks something off his shoulder.*

What?

GWEN: You just had some lint.

> *A beat. His phone rings.*

Oh. Your phone.

THEO: Oh!

> *He answers.*

Hello? Oh, hi. How are you? Mm-hm. Oh. Okay. Yeah, no, no problem. Don't worry about it. Alrighty. You take care. Okay. Bye.

GWEN: Who was that?

THEO: My dentist.

GWEN: Your dentist?

THEO: Yeah. I need a root canal.

GWEN: Oh no! That sucks.

THEO: What can you do? Getting older, eh? He's going to call me later to schedule it.

GWEN: I hope everything's okay.

THEO: It'll be fine. *(Beat. About someone offstage.)* Look.

GWEN: Adorable.

THEO: I hope I'm still holding someone's hand at that age. How long do you think they've been together?

GWEN: They've got to be in their eighties. Maybe decades.

THEO: Or maybe they met later in life.

GWEN: I guess they could've. Oh, he's wiping off the bench for her. I love that.

THEO: Do you think someone could have more than one soulmate?

GWEN: Sure. There's billions of people in the world. *(She turns and hollers.)* WELCOME BACK, SURVIVORS! BE SURE TO COLLECT YOUR LOOT BEFORE YOU DISEMBARK! AND PLEASE CONSIDER RATING US ON YEEEEELLP! *(To him.)* My apologies.

THEO: Look how happy they all look. It must be a great tour.

GWEN: People seem to like it. Don't look so glum. There's still the seven o'clock.

                Her phone rings.

                What is that? Is that your phone again?

THEO: Nope. I think it's coming from your...

GWEN: What?

THEO: Your...breastal area.

GWEN:	Oh, crap. *(She fishes her cell phone out of her bra.)* Who the hell is calling me? I forgot this thing even had a ringer. Hello? Stuart... Sorry, Stuart who? Oh, Mr. Stuart! Yes, now I recognize it from my paycheque. Uh, how can I help you? Oh. I see. Okay. No problem. Thanks.
THEO:	Everything okay?
GWEN:	That was my boss. They didn't sell enough tickets for tonight so they're cancelling the seven o'clock tour. I'm sorry.
THEO:	Oh. That's...par for the course, I guess.

He moans.

GWEN:	Paramedic?
THEO:	I'm fine.
GWEN:	You still have your date with Erica to look forward to. It looks like a nice evening for a walk.
THEO:	Erica's not coming.
GWEN:	Yes, she is, Theo.
THEO:	No, in fact, she's not. That was her that called.
GWEN:	What?
THEO:	I told you it was my dentist.
GWEN:	You lied?
THEO:	Yeah.
GWEN:	Why?
THEO:	I...guess I didn't want you to feel bad for me.

GWEN: I do feel bad for you! Why did she cancel?

THEO: The ferry's still down. And it turns out she met someone while waiting. They're going to go paddle boating.

GWEN: Oh shit.

THEO: Yeah. It's okay, though, honestly. The worst part is I actually really wanted to hear the story.

GWEN: The Woman in White?

THEO: Yeah. It's up my alley, that's the truth. I was going to go even if she never showed.

GWEN: Really?

THEO: I want to know more about this woman. Who was she? What happened to her? Why did she throw herself into the river?

GWEN: That would make you happy? Hearing the story?

THEO: It would make me happier.

               A long beat. GWEN starts digging in the kiosk.

               What are you doing?

               GWEN comes out with a script in her hand.

GWEN: "His cheek and brow in moonlight shone

               Fair as the horse he rode upon

               She watched, the woman all in white

               Her heart was lost that very night—"

THEO: What is that? What are you reading?

GWEN: You want to go on the tour?

THEO: Yes, but—

GWEN: I'm taking you on the tour. Please take a seat. It gets rocky out here on the open water.

THEO: Gwen, you don't have to—

GWEN: Please hold your questions till the end. And no flash photography. *(She pretends to address other passengers.)* Ma'am? Ma'am? Is that tuna fish? I think we'd all appreciate if you didn't. Sir, please remove your enormous hat. The people behind you can't see. No chewing gum, young lady. Put that under the seat. And you, sir. *(Addressing THEO.)* I just wanted to say, I like your shoes.

> *A beat. She pulls off the wool skirt and is now in the petticoat. Ideally this puts her all in white.*

THEO: Whoa. The skirt is coming off.

> *As GWEN recites, she begins to embody the poem.*

GWEN: "His cheek and brow in moonlight shone

Fair as the horse he rode upon

She watched, the woman all in white

Her heart was lost that very night

He to another was espoused

To make good on his father's vow

And yet her lips he visited

No care that they would never wed

He lay her in the field of snow

What was between them overflow'd

And still, he married in the spring

The bluebirds singing tring-a-ling

The bride a vision 'neath her veil

Two cheeks like roses, two so pale

She caught the bunch of marigold

Though in the sun, her heart turned cold

The couple honeymoon'd abroad

They built a home on ground untrod

And yet she loved his golden cheek

Seen from afar, her vision weak

Each time she saw him with his bride

She felt more hollow deep inside

The years no salve upon her soul

One day she climbed the stony knoll

O'er the river that fed the lake

Her mortal coil she would forsake

A tumbling glance, the purest white

Beneath the water, out of sight

The lake flowed on towards the sea

A wraith, upon the waves was she

For without him she would not live

And yet her soul would never give

And so she's there both day and night

The tragic woman all in white."

She finishes. A long beat.

Well, there you have it. You've been on the tour.

THEO: She threw herself into the river over him? That kind of makes me mad.

GWEN: What?

THEO: That's what she died for? A guy who chose someone else?

GWEN: He didn't choose.

THEO: He married in the spring, after laying her in the snow.

GWEN: To make good on his father's vow.

THEO: His father's vow? Who cares? If he loved her—

GWEN: Fate forced them apart. That's how it goes sometimes.

THEO: So she threw it all away?

GWEN: She couldn't live without him.

THEO: No, she could. She just chose not to. She gave up.

GWEN: She didn't give up. Her heart broke.

THEO: Maybe because she spent all her time pining. Maybe if she'd gotten out—

GWEN: Yeah, she probably should have gone to more barn dances.

THEO: I'm just saying—

GWEN: I've got to close up.

THEO: Oh. Right. No seven o'clock.

                She starts to close up. He cleans up his things.

GWEN: Nope. Off a few hours early. I should get to the airport with time to spare.

THEO: You're leaving tonight?

GWEN: Yeah. Red-eye.

THEO: I never sleep on those.

GWEN: Me neither.

THEO: So, where are you starting?

GWEN: Hm?

THEO: Your travels. Where to first?

GWEN: Italy.

THEO: Really?

GWEN: Yeah.

THEO: You didn't want to go somewhere new? Somewhere you've never seen?

GWEN: I wanted to see the sea again.

THEO: And then where?

GWEN: Then where what?

THEO: After Italy. You must have pre-booked your flights. Your trains. Your hotels. Where do you go after you see the sea?

GWEN:	Nowhere. Just Italy.
THEO:	Just Italy. So, when you said you were going to travel, you meant you were going to Italy.
GWEN:	Yeah. Doesn't that count as travel?
THEO:	How long are you staying?
GWEN:	What's with all these questions?
THEO:	I'm just asking.
GWEN:	What are you asking?

A beat.

THEO:	How long has it been since your husband died, again? Was it two years tomorrow?

A long beat.

GWEN:	I've got to go. This was…nice, Theo.
THEO:	Gwen.
GWEN:	What?
THEO:	This was nice. It was more than nice.

Another long beat.

GWEN:	You're staring.
THEO:	I know what you're going to Italy to do.
GWEN:	That's because I told you. I'm going to see the sea.
THEO:	Yeah? And what's after that? You didn't tell me that.
GWEN:	Whatever's beyond the sea.
THEO:	Jesus.

GWEN:	What?
THEO:	Look, I know you might be feeling—
GWEN:	You don't know how I'm feeling.
THEO:	I do a little.
GWEN:	Your wife left you for a hipster. My husband went down in a helicopter. It's not the same.
THEO:	No, it's not. But, you know, at the end of the day, we're in the same boat. We both have to start over. Move on. Isn't that what we just talked about?
GWEN:	You move on, Theo. I want you to have a good life.
THEO:	And you?
GWEN:	I gave it an honest try.
THEO:	Why? Because you gave it two years?
GWEN:	Yes.
THEO:	It's a totally arbitrary period of time. Maybe you need more.
GWEN:	That's all I ever promised him.
THEO:	What about other people? Don't you have people that would—
GWEN:	What? Grieve? No. I've made very sure of that. No one will mourn. No one's world will stop. No one will even be inconvenienced. I live in a town where no one knows me and I do a job that matters to no one.
THEO:	Earlier you said everything we do has an impact.

GWEN: I meant on the earth.

She checks that she's done everything.

Have a good night, Theo. And take care of yourself.

She starts to head off.

THEO: Wait. Answer this question. Right after Nate died, would you have noticed that fox?

GWEN: What?

THEO: The fox we saw earlier. Would you have noticed her a few weeks after Nate died?

GWEN: Probably not. Why?

THEO: Because it made you happy to see her. For a minute. Maybe not all day. But for minute you felt something you couldn't have felt back then. So something has gotten better. And I don't think that was the only time today. You brushed a piece of lint off my shoulder.

GWEN: So?

THEO: So, I don't think there was any lint. I spent a long time with a lint brush this morning. I think you touched me, because for a moment you wanted to feel another person. And you know what? I felt that in my entire body. You think your life means nothing to anyone? This wasn't nothing to me. I know it was only a little while, and I know we barely know each other. I'm not saying I'm your soulmate, but it wasn't nothing. So, if that's the thing you're using to comfort yourself, I'm sorry to tell you I'm going to think about today for a long time. And it's going to mean something to me. When I met you, I was terrified about my date with Erica, but that was nothing compared to how scared I was when I saw her calling and thought she was on her way. Because I didn't want to stop talking to you. I'll tell you what's beyond the sea, Gwen. Something beautiful. And it's waiting for us. But not yet. Not now. Look, I don't know what I'm doing either. But I'm going to keep waking up every morning. Because some days you meet someone like you.

> *The sound of ducks. GWEN turns her back to the audience to look at them. A long beat. THEO goes to stands beside her. He reaches out his hand. Beat. She takes it. She crumples into him.*
>
> *End of play.*

Glossary / Background Information

The Woman in White: Women-in-white ghost stories exist across many cultures and often share a common theme of tragedy and love gone wrong.

Trevi Fountain: A large 18th-century fountain in the Piazza di Trevi, Rome, Italy, which depicts the Roman God of the sea, Neptune.

Ostia: A settlement on the sea near Rome.

Gilbert Blythe: A character in Lucy Maude Montgomery's Anne of Green Gables series.

Wasaga Beach: A popular summer tourist destination in Ontario, Canada.

Canada's Wonderland: A large amusement park in Vaughan, Ontario which once included a water ride called Zumba Flume which was retired in 1994.

Witness in Time: A fictional series of novels invented for this play.